Art Nouveau Designs

Coloring Book

Alphonse Marie Mucha

Rendered by
Ed Sibbett, Jr.

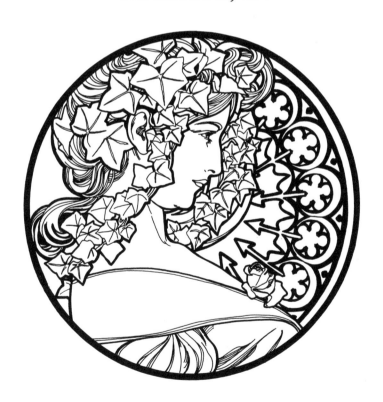

Dover Publications, Inc.
Mineola, New York

Between the years 1895 and 1904—the heart of the Belle Époque—French poster and decorative art was dominated by the Moravian artist Alphonse Marie Mucha (1860–1939). Mucha's style—originally dubbed simply *le style Mucha,* rather than the now familiar term Art Nouveau—was best known for its strong and sensuous line, elaborate hairstyles and drapery, mosaic patterns, and the use of halos. Thirty-one of Muchas illustrations have been carefully rendered for coloring by noted artist and illustrator Ed Sibbett, Jr. The detailed designs will provide artists and colorists with endless possibilities for experimentation with color and technique. Plus, perforated pages make displaying your work easy.

Bibliographical Note

Art Nouveau Designs Coloring Book, first published by Dover Publications, Inc., in 2015, contains a selection of plates from *The Mucha Poster Coloring Book,* originally published by Dover in 1977, and reprinted in 1985 as *Art Nouveau Figurative Designs.*

International Standard Book Number

ISBN-13: 978-0-486-78189-1
ISBN-10: 0-486-78189-5

Manufactured in the United States by RR Donnelley
78189501   2015
www.doverpublications.com

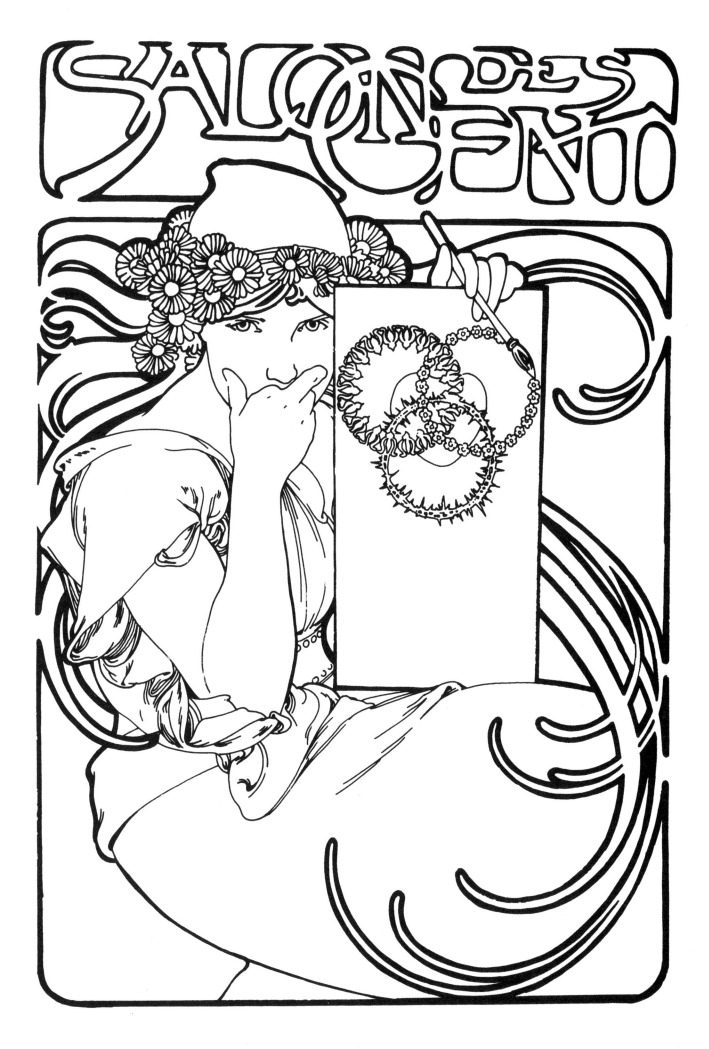

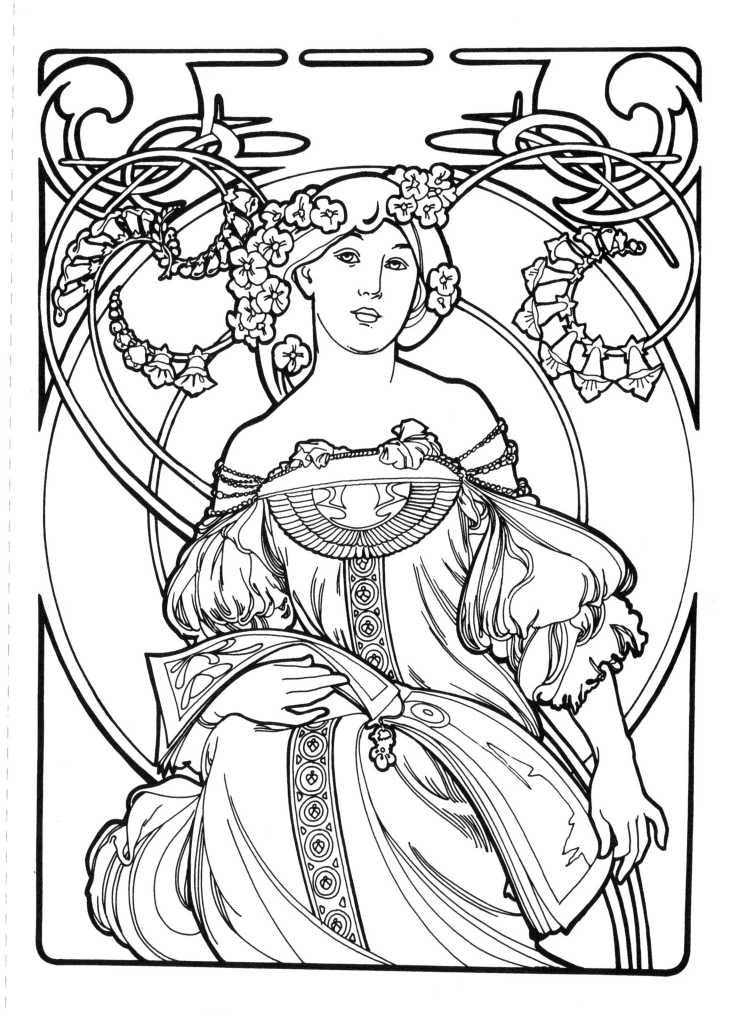

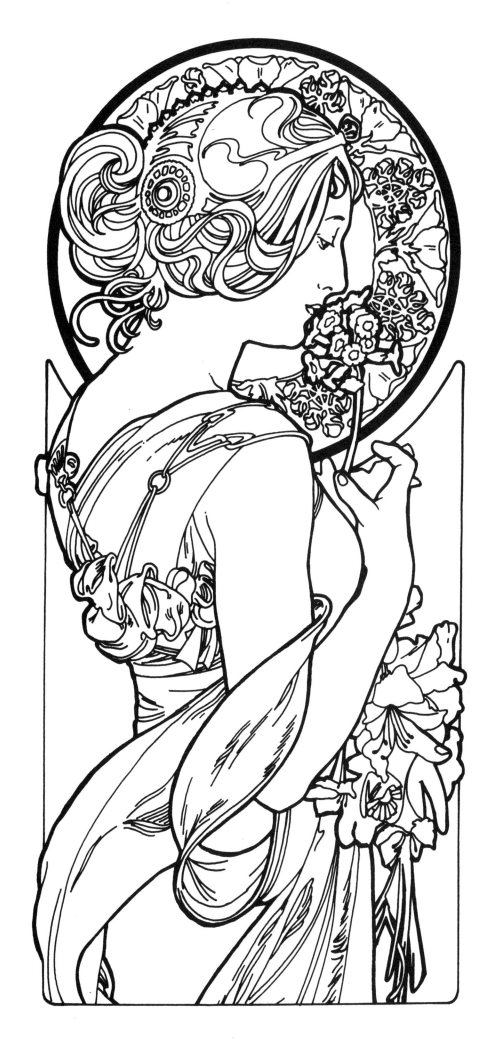

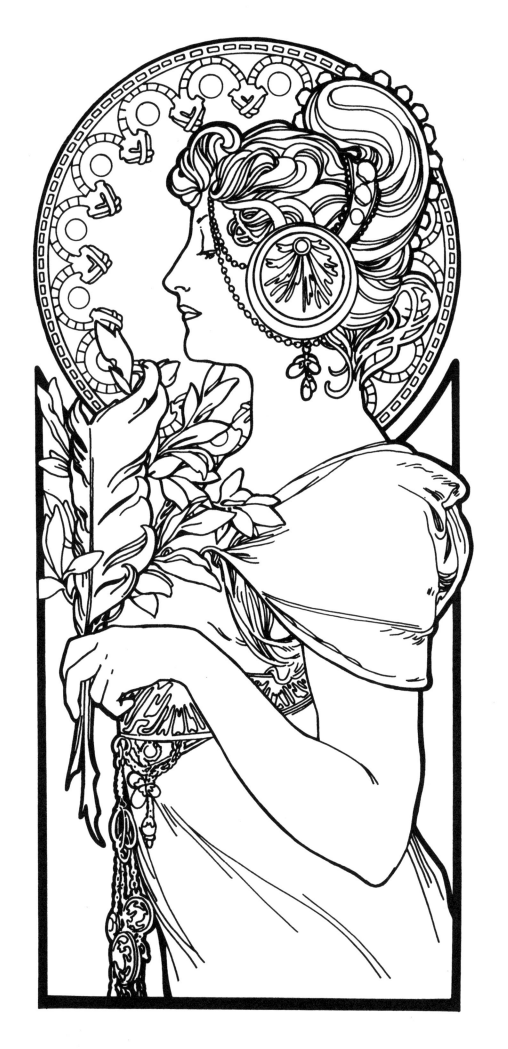

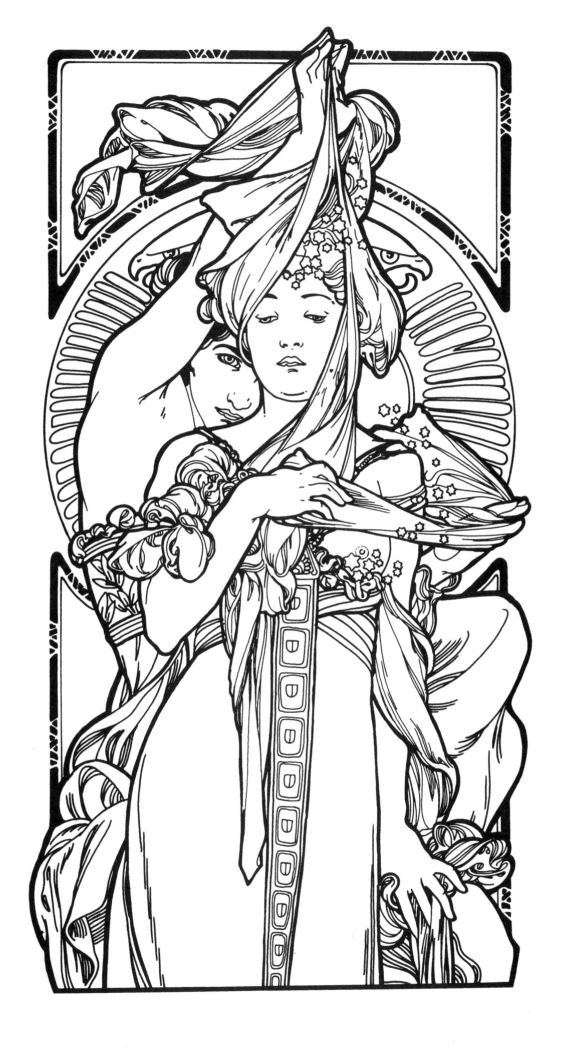

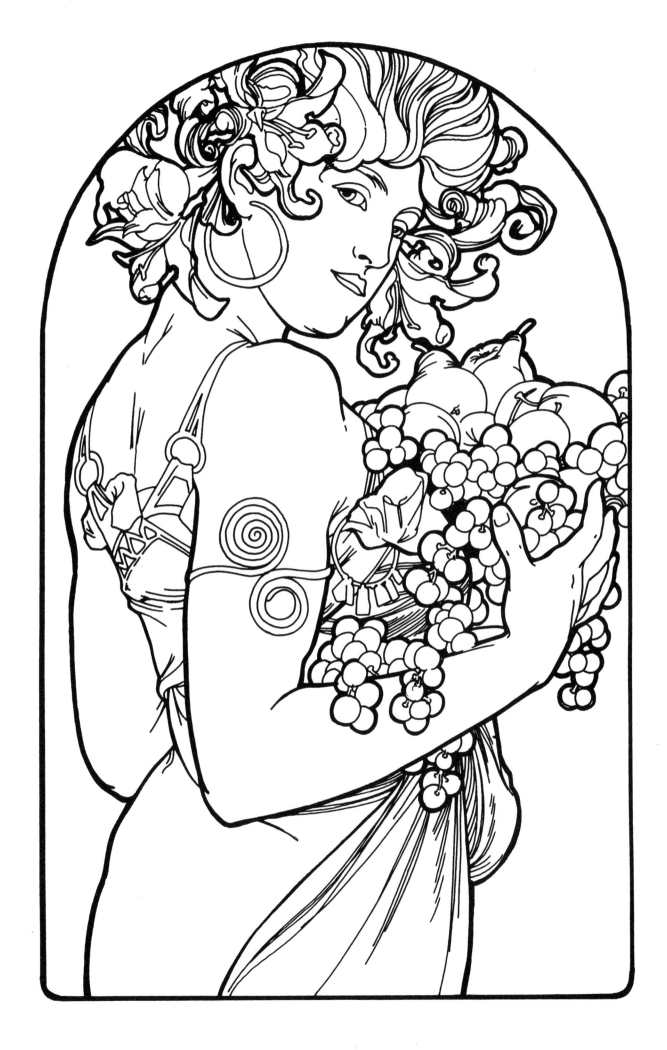

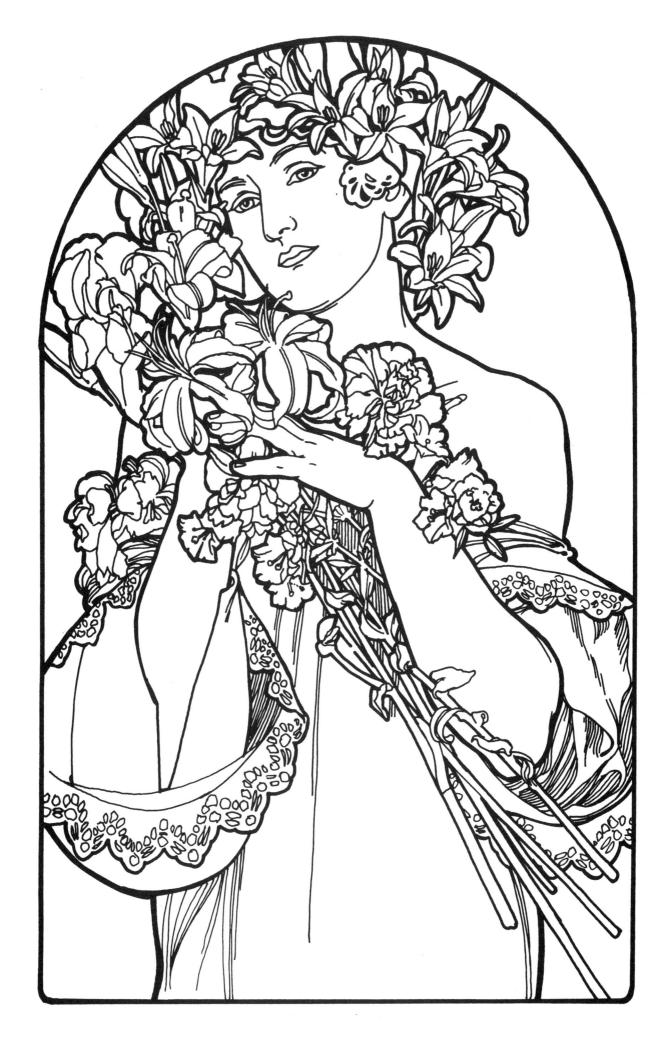

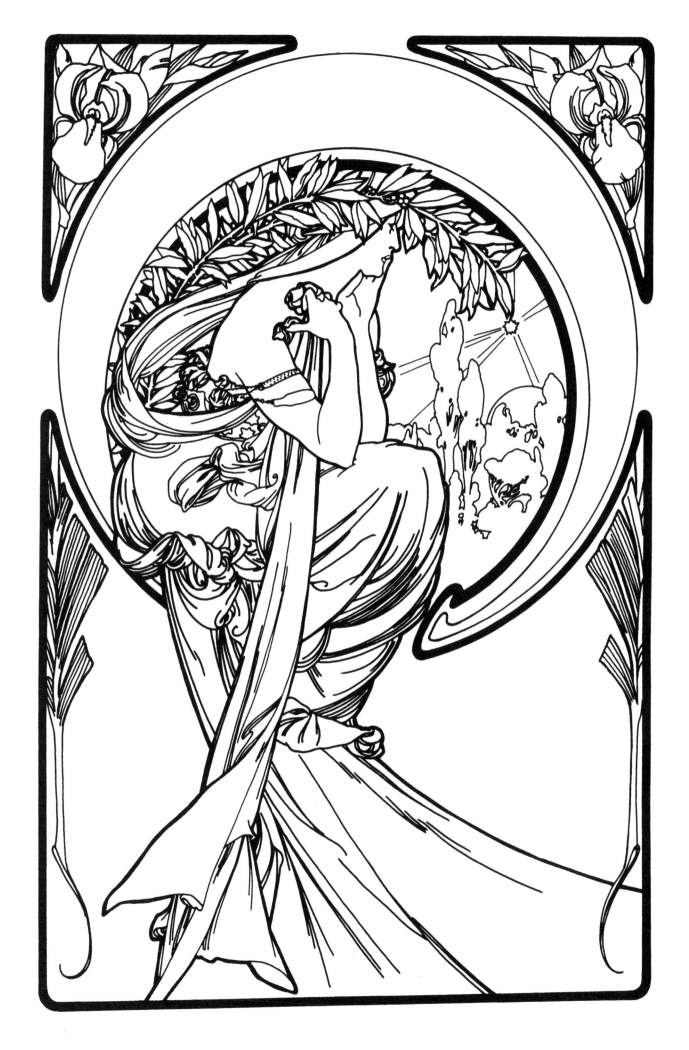

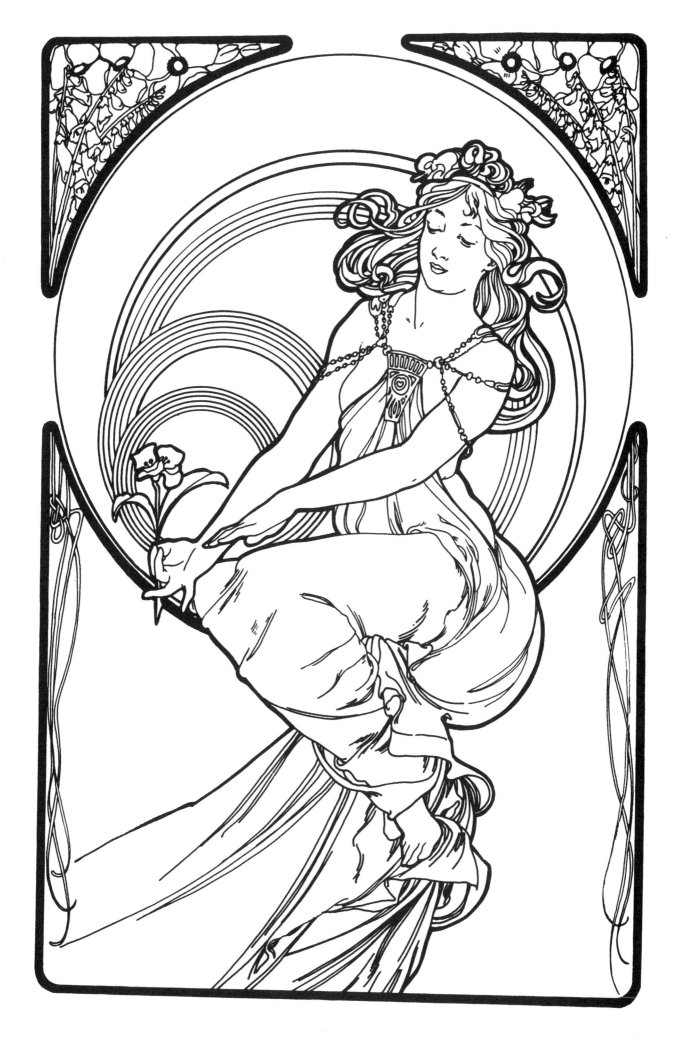

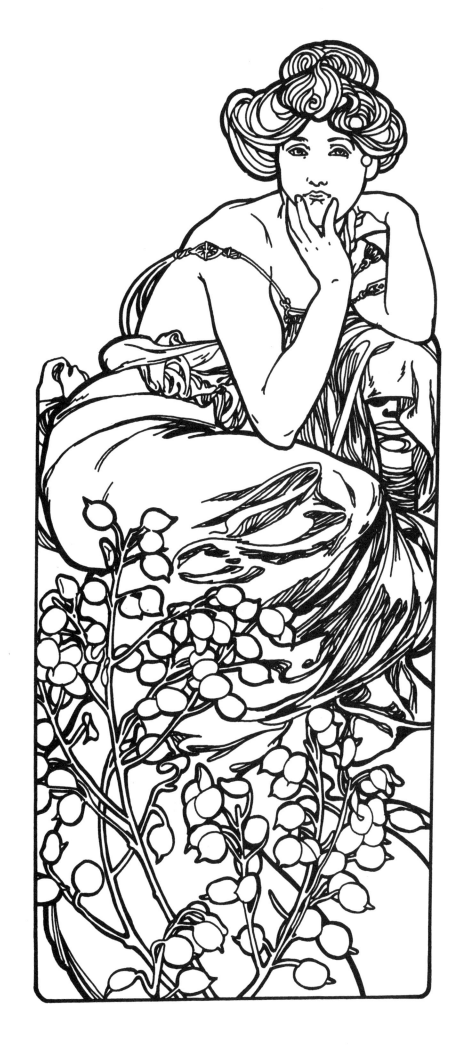

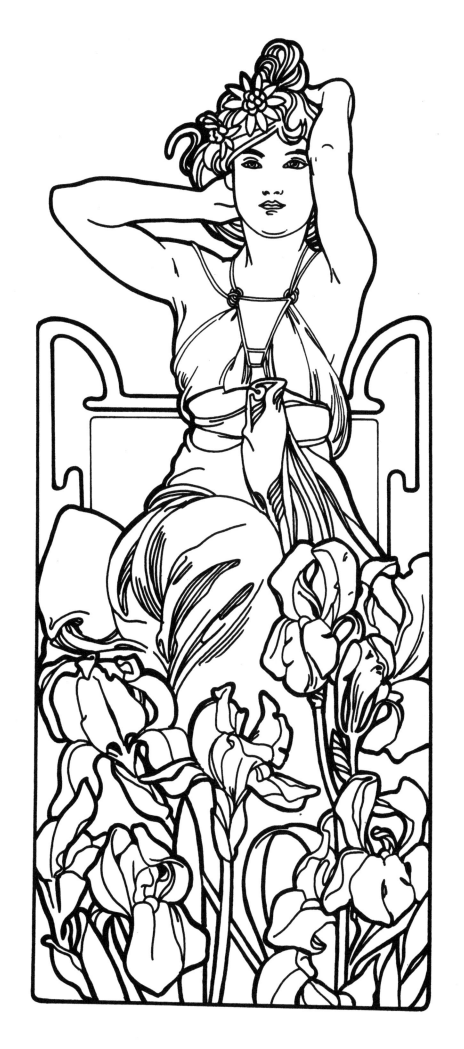

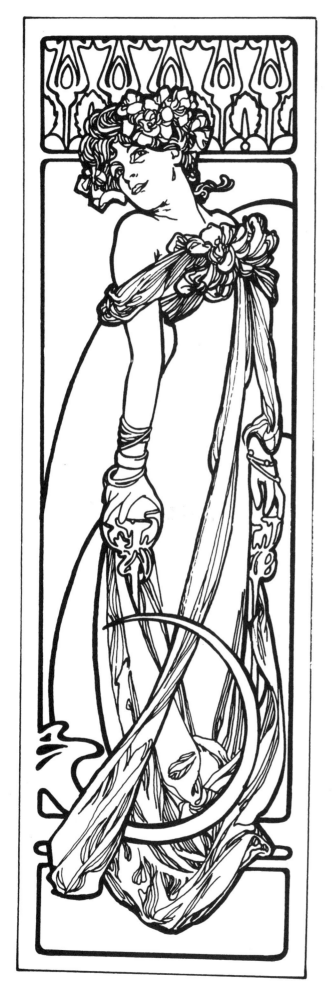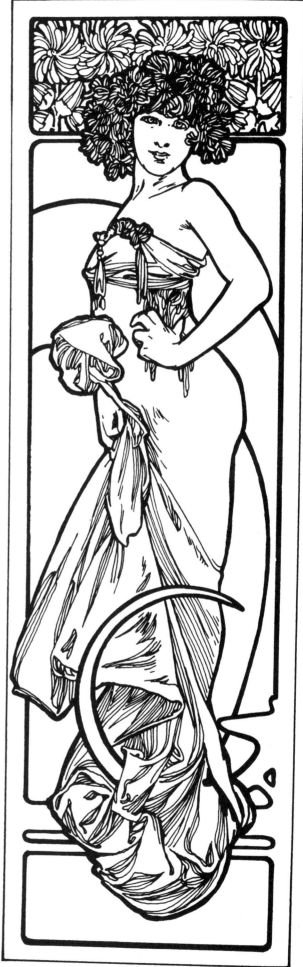

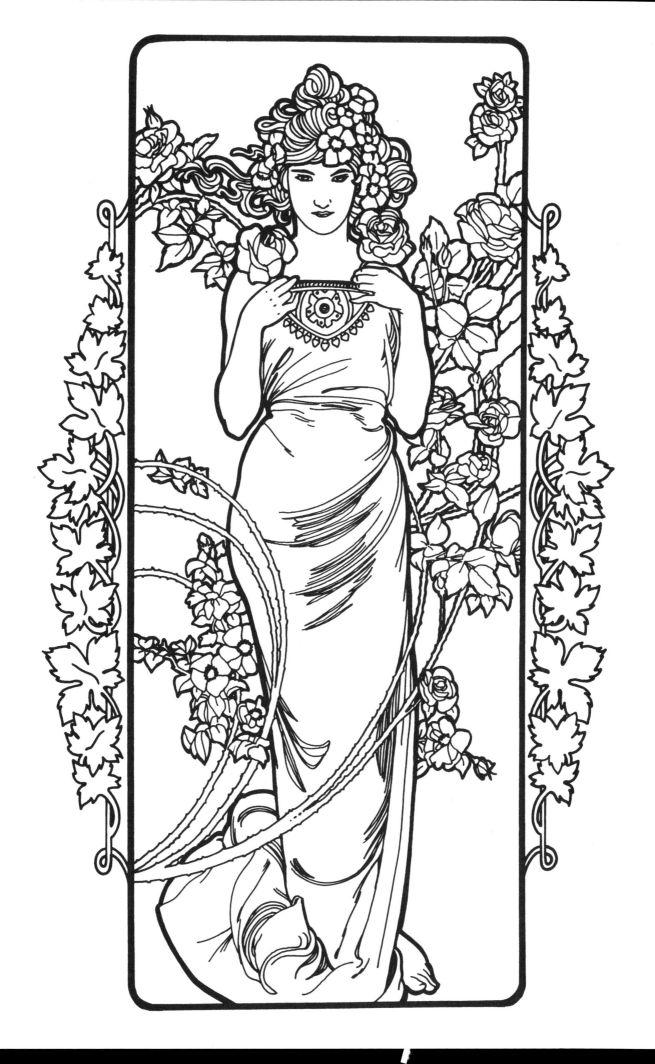

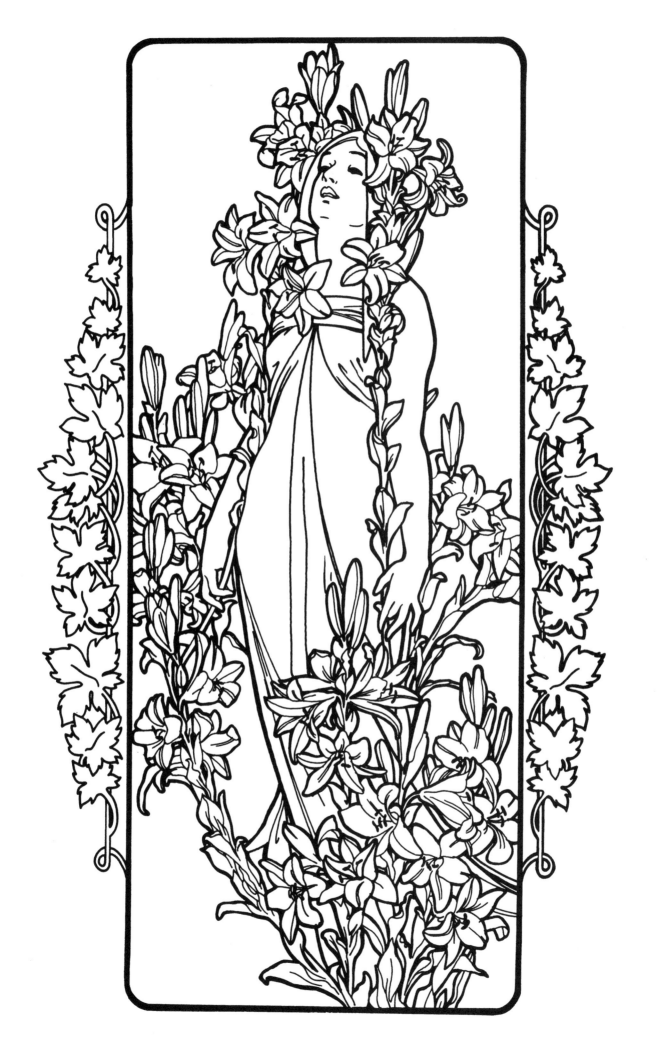

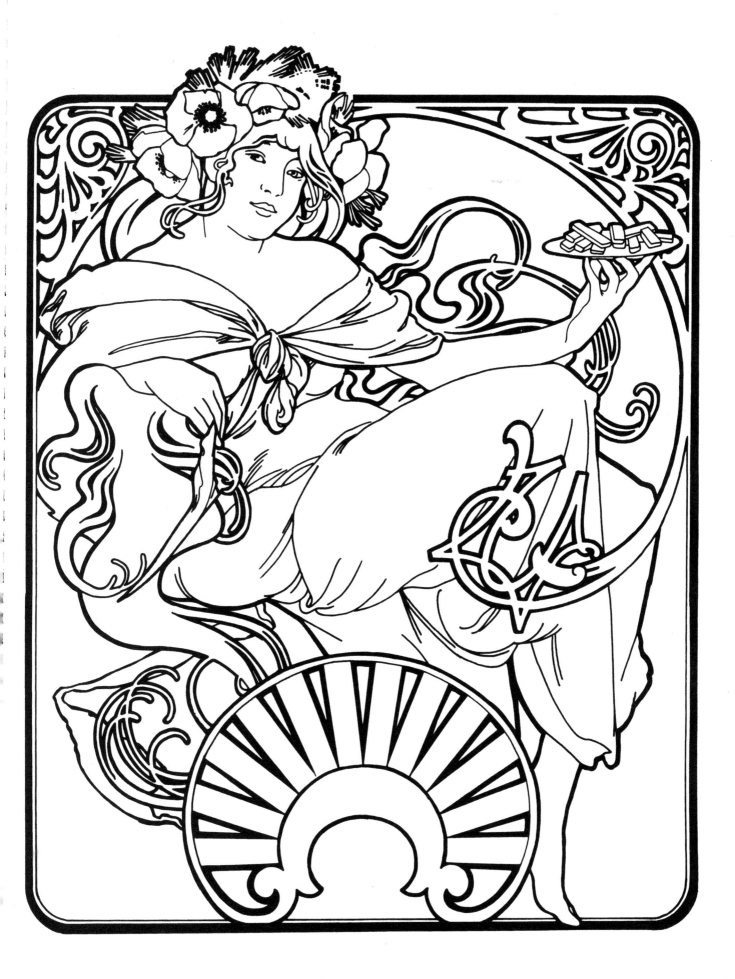

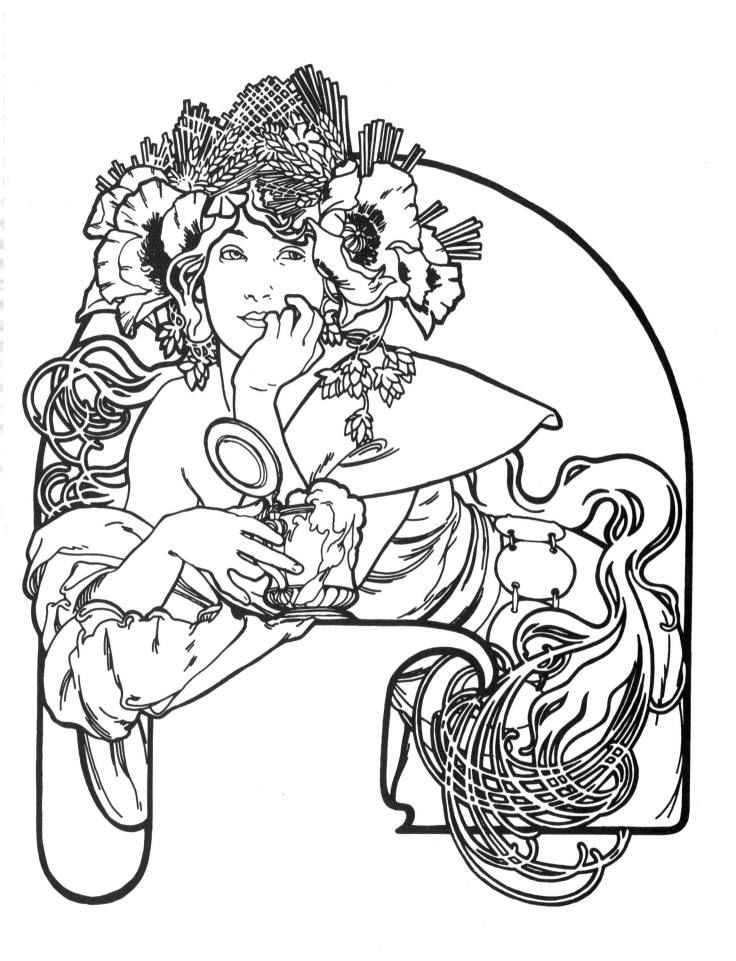

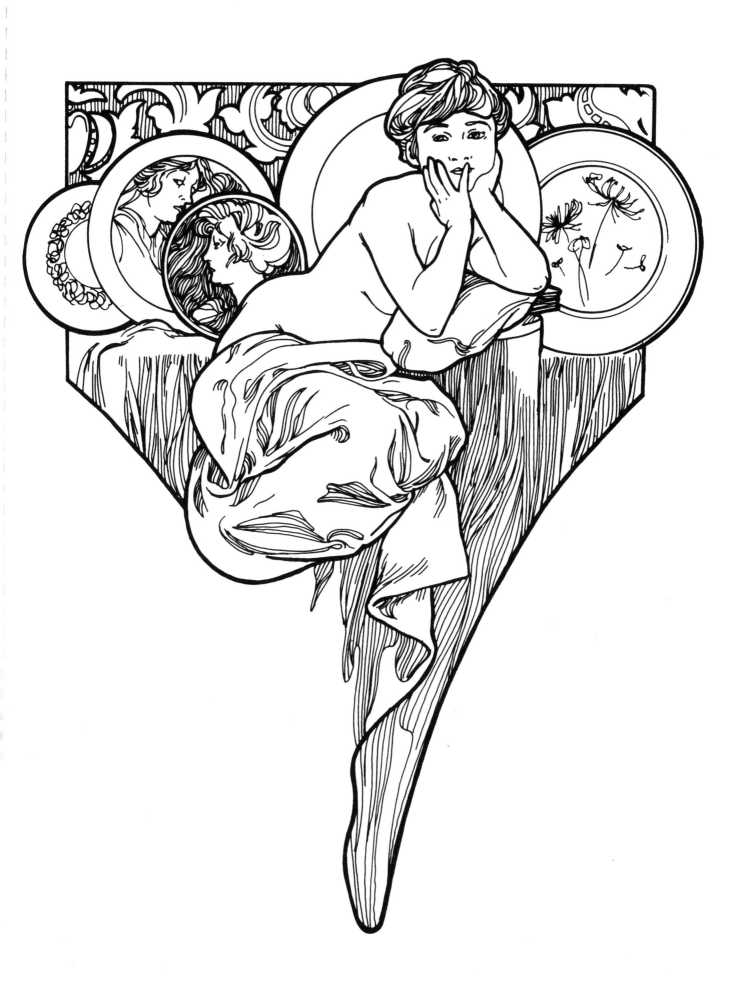

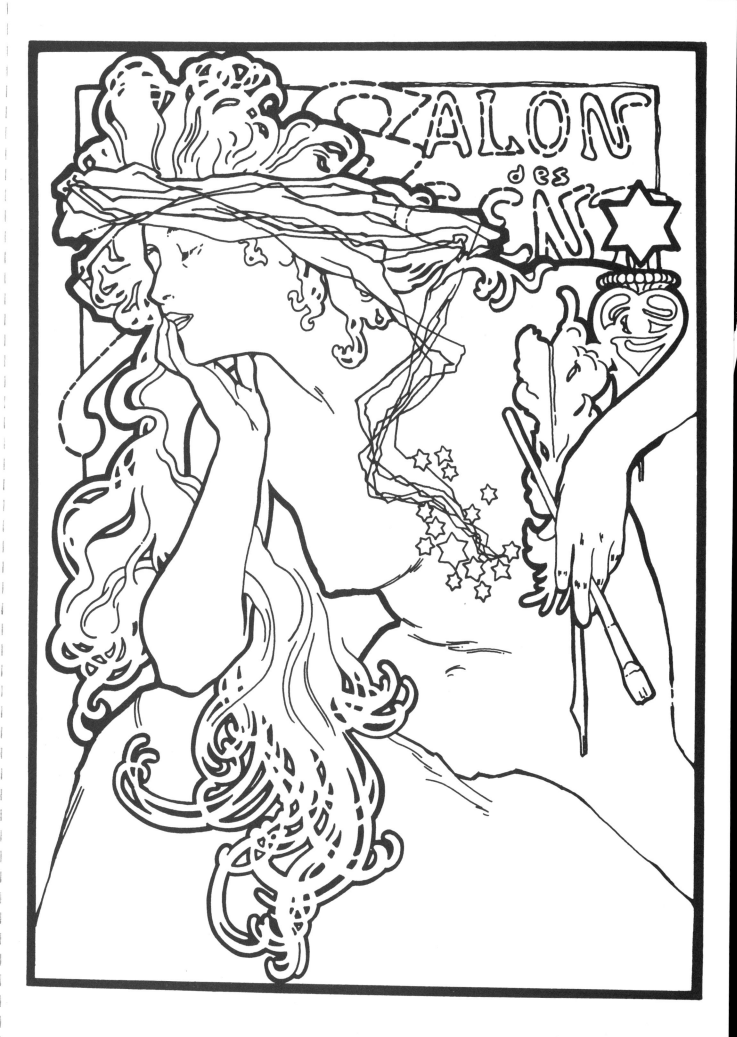

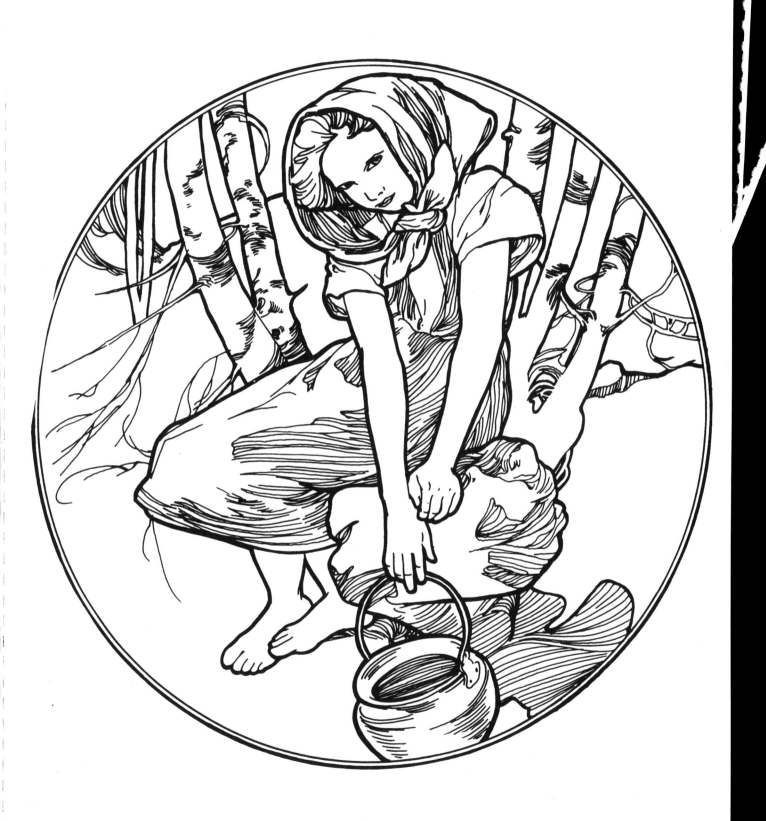

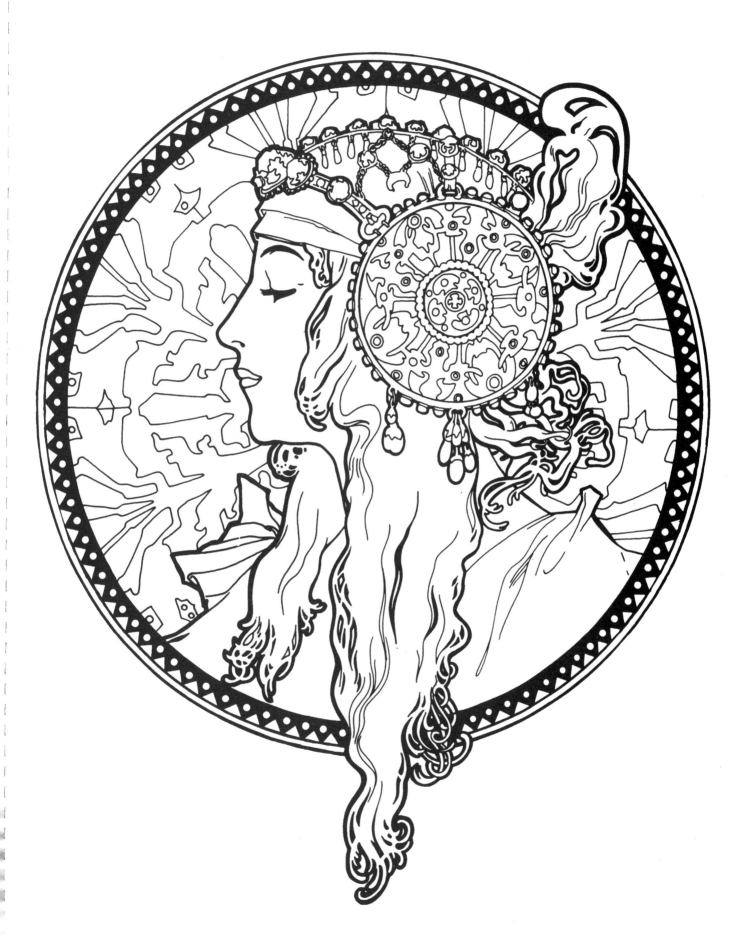

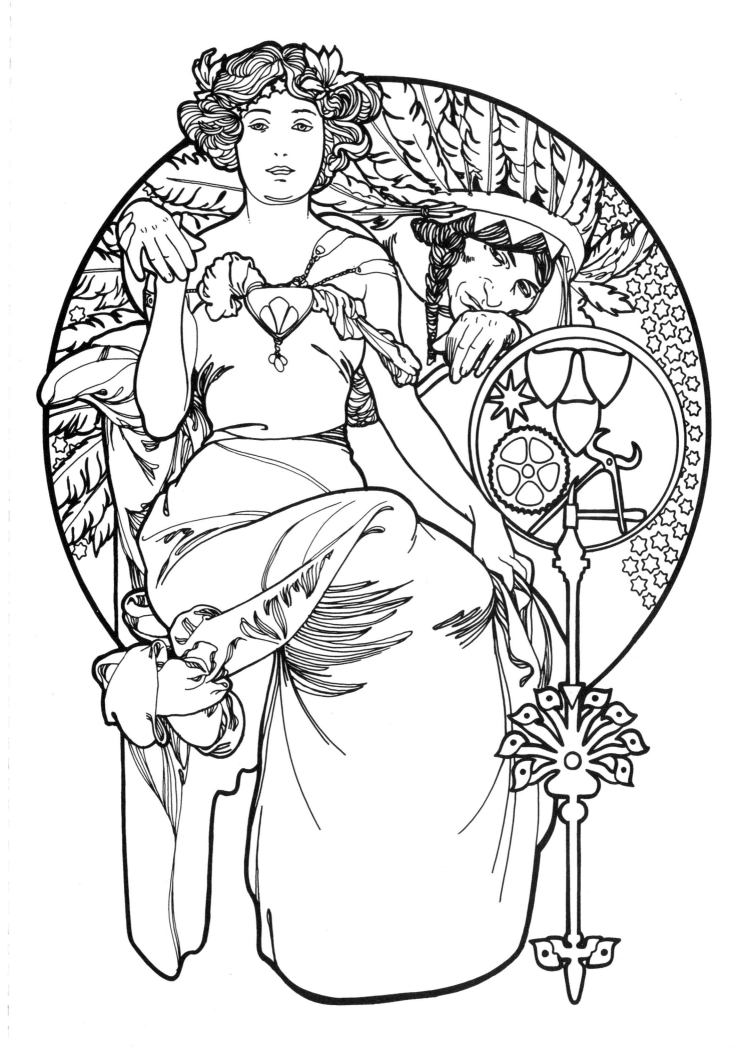

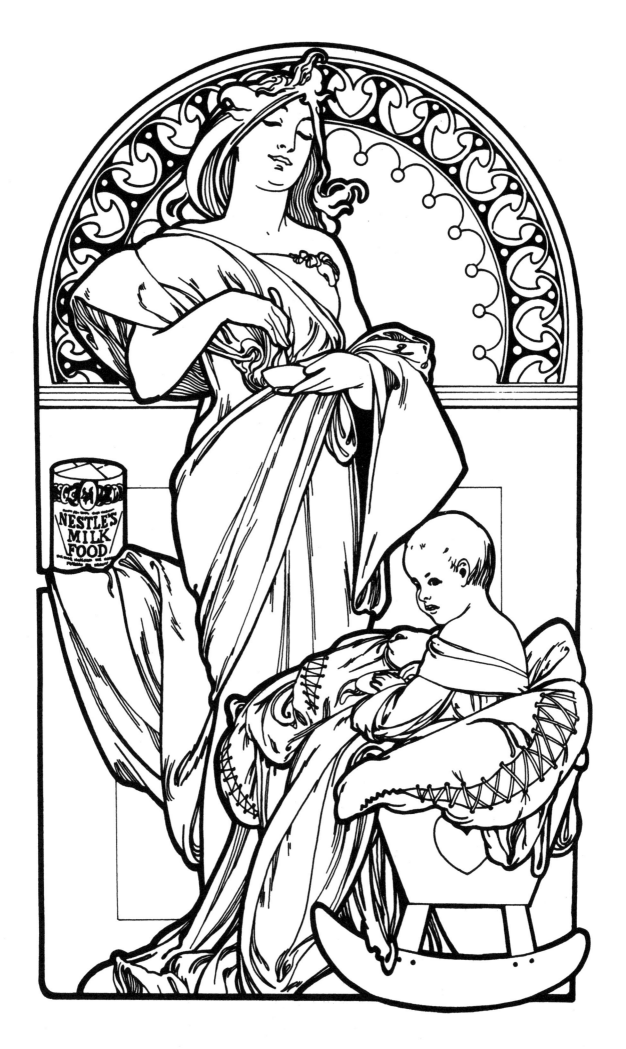

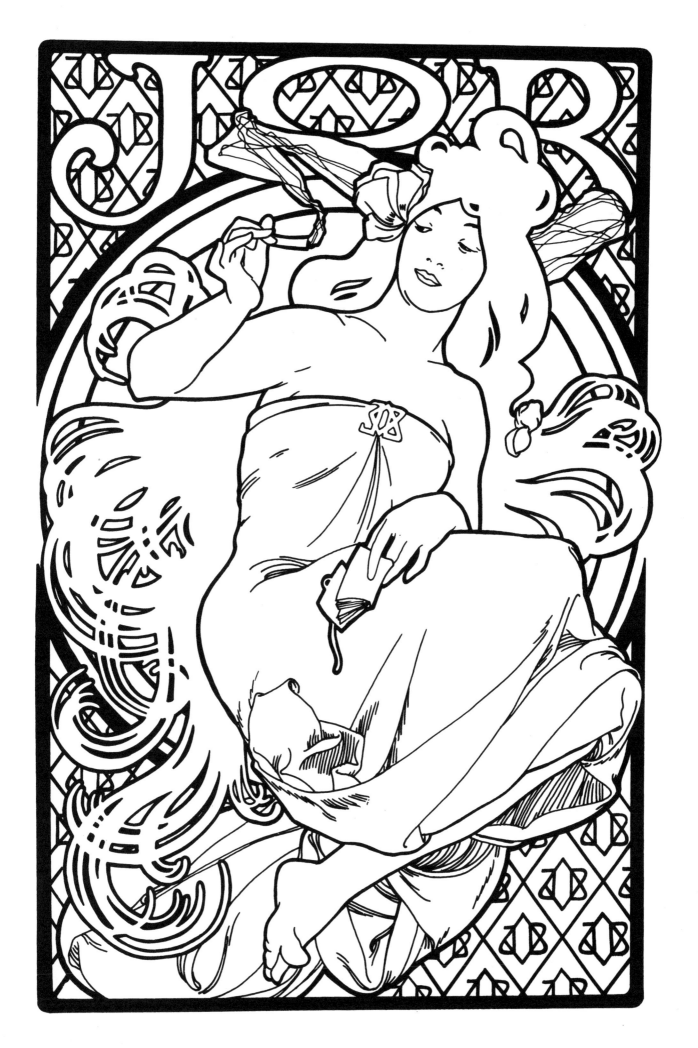

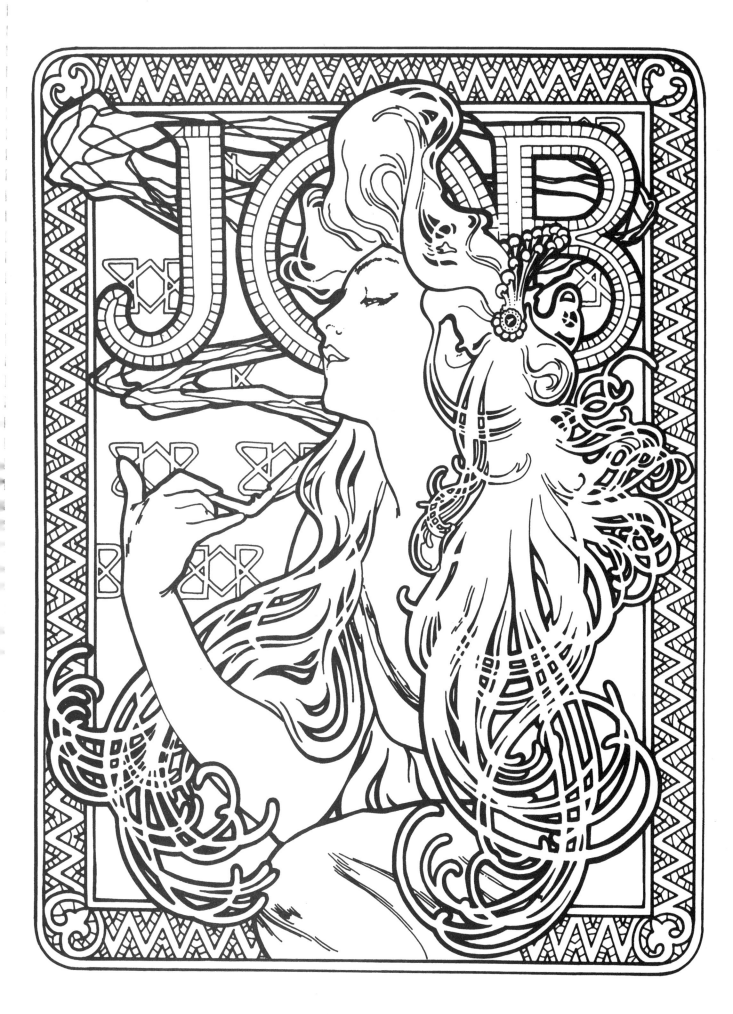

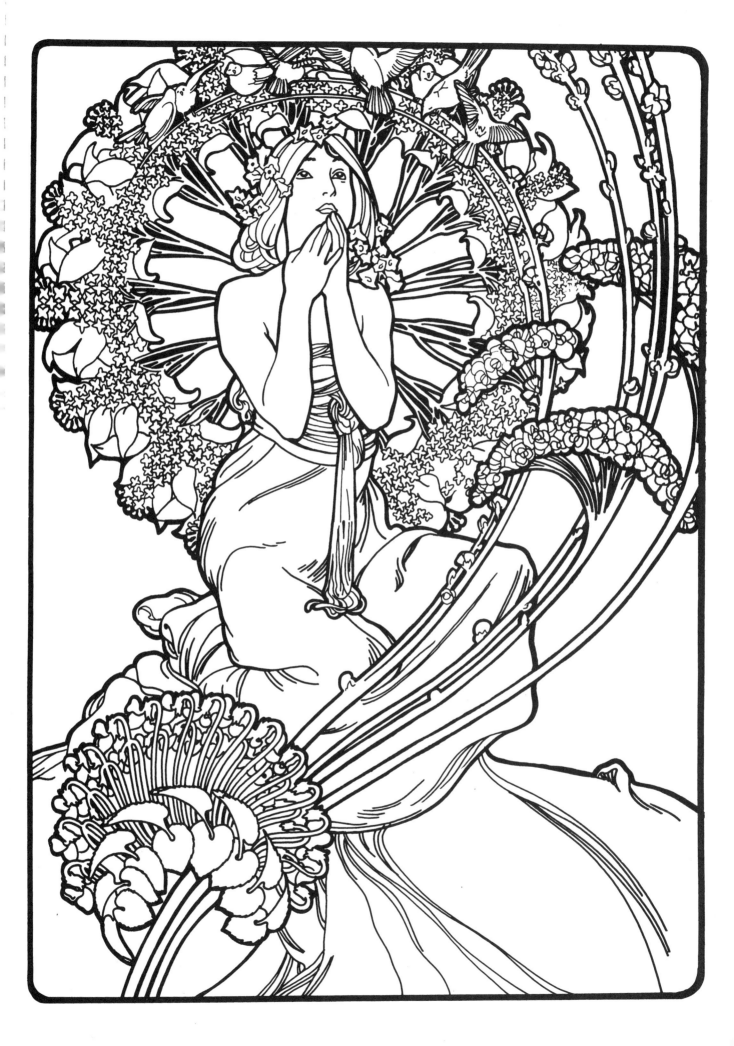

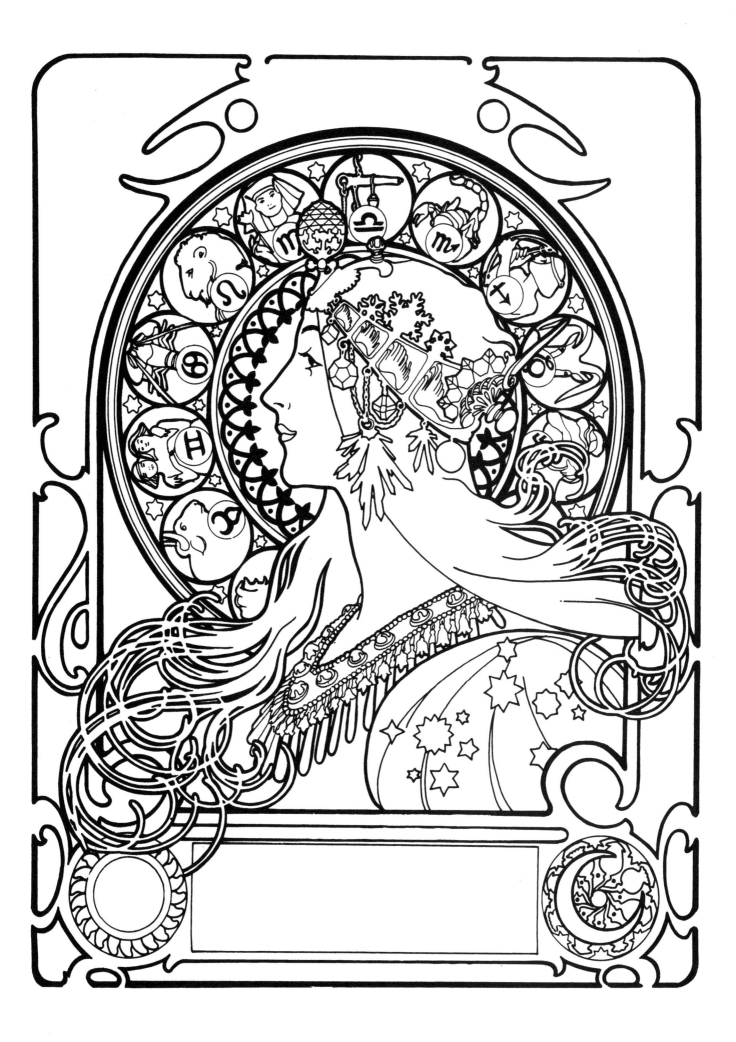